S.O.A.R
Sounds of A Revolution

Nefarious J. Dorsey

Author's Signature Page

Acknowledgments

I want to thank my mother, the late Floried R. Tindall-Dorsey, who was also a Poet, and helped nourish my gift from an early age. I want to thank my siblings, Keith Dorsey, Aaron Dorsey, the late Paul Dorsey, Marcia Dorsey, and Dr. Leslie C. Dorsey. Special thanks to my children, **ShaNay**, Mariah, Myriko and Gavin. I love you very much and am better because of you.

I want to thank my mentors Dr. Tina Jordan, and Kiti Fowlkes.

Finally, Cryss A. Jones, of Collective Press, for overseeing this project from concept and content creation, Branding, and Edits, to Literary Consultation, thank you.

.

Contents

The America I Know

SLAVE SHIPS EQUIPPED
WITH PRECIOUS CARGO
BLACK HOLES FOR BLACK SOULS
THIS IS THE AMERICA THAT I KNOW

THE EMANCIPATION PROCLAMATION
DIVIDED THIS NATION
AND IS THE REASON WHY
LINCOLN WAS ASSASSINATED
SEE THE CIVIL WAR WAS
ABOUT SLAVERY
AND IT WAS BLACK SOLDIER'S
BRAVERY
THAT SAW THE NORTH WIN
AS A NEW CHAPTER
IN AMERICAN HISTORY BEGINS

THIS IS THE AMERICA I KNOW

FROM 3/5 TO THIS
SEE, ROSA PARK
SPARKED THE MOVEMENT
AS MARTIN CALLED
FOR IMPROVEMENTS
IN RACE RELATIONS
CHALLENGING THIS NATION
TO BE GREAT
NON-VIOLENTLY DEFYING HATE
AS HISTORY SHOWS

THIS IS THE AMERICA THAT I KNOW

AN HISTORIC ELECTION
CHANGED THE DIRECTION
AND FOR ONCE COMPLEXION
DIDN'T PLAY A PART
AS PEOPLE VOTED
WITH THEIR HEARTS
SO IT GOES TO SHOW
THAT THE AMERICA I KNOW
HAS CHANGED?

Burn Baltimore Burn

I know why I am hated
Because I am so opinionated
I supported the ones who are
Frustrated
To a degree but listen
To me clearly
Looting and shooting
On our side of town
I have found to be ludacris
Because the point you always
Miss
You may not want to
Pump your fist to this
But think logically
Because what I see
Is that America only
Understands
Violence and money
So when I say
Burn Baltimore Burn
They all must learn
It is maybe because I am a
60's baby and
That the only way to stop it
Is to hit them in their pockets
So don't burn down the side
Of town that is the poorest
Hit them where the tourist
Spend all of their money

See,
If you mess with their revenue
They are more inclined
To listen to you
So here is what we need
To do
Against Baltimore City
And the Boys in Blue
Target the Inner Harbor
And Camden Yards
Make it harder for them
To make a dollar
Watch them scream and
Holler
Watch the truth surface
Because looting and shooting
In our neighborhoods
Serves no purpose
So learn why Baltimore
Needs to burn
Because the DOJ*
Constantly allows
Them to get away
With killing Black Men
It is time that this comes
To an end
See, for me
Nothing can be more sweeter
Than to unload my 9 millimeter
As you
Feel my rage coming from my
12 gauge shotgun
They must pay for what
They have done
As too many mothers have
Buried their sons
So we must even the
Score in Baltimore
So the world must learn
Why Baltimore has to burn

- Department of Justice

Open Season

Trayvon is gone
Now who is next
On the hit list?
As clenched fist
React to this
Ferguson
Is murdering
One of our sons
Again
When will the
Legal executions
End?
4 shots in the arm and
2 to the head
The end result is
Michael Brown
Is Dead
There's no reason
For it to be
Open Season
Again and again
When will it end?
Trayvon is gone
And now
Michael Brown is too
What in the hell are
We going to do?

Middle finger to the law
We know what the fuck
We saw
Saw that same bullshit
In the sunshine state
Can you now relate?
Molotov cocktails
Fail to get our point across
How many lives have been
Lost?
In this Holocaust
What is the actual cost?
In fact, how many more Blacks
Must die
Leaving us to wonder why
That the only reason
For Open Season
Resides in extermination
And genocide

Juneteenth

Right now, Juneteenth
Has me sucking my teeth
Like I got some beef
Stuck in them
It's a celebration of what?
And what for?
When we are in the middle
Of a race war
As the Emancipation Proclamation
Changed the nation and led
To the assassination of Lincoln
Though the news was delayed
By a few years in Texas
You can expect this as
A quiet riot still falls on deaf ears
And hasn't disappeared
Yet,
I have deep regrets
As the music of justice
They have chosen
Not to hear
Unlike Paul Revere
The message is still the same
It's loud and clear
They don't want us here
See, the news got misconstrued
Causing a bigger issue
As soldiers fighting in the Northern
Army was supposed to be free
Ensuring a victory over the South
Because the war was about
Slavery
So feel free to fact check me
As I put a wrinkle in the history
Because the tapestry has been
Sewn up with lies
That is why
Juneteenth has me sucking

My teeth
Like I got some beef
Stuck in them
Still I am seeking relief
Because I need a toothpick
To unstick and dislodge
The bullshit because I am
Not having it
As the walls of Black Wallstreet
Came tumbling down to the ground
As the town burned only to learn
That misinformation was the causation
Of the worst massacre in U.S. history
And yet years later
You celebrate that we are free
Why are we celebrating when they
Are still hating as the race baiting
Continues
I thought you knew that the issues
Are not new they have been renewed
Juneteenth celebrates a lie
That will not dissipate
Under the disguise that we
Have been freed from slavery
Yet, we still behave like slaves
Because if you look you will
See that the premise is faulty
Because today we are
Still not free!

Safe Poem

This poem is for the people
Who have perfect lives
The housewives
Whose husbands are
Making the bacon
While they stay at home
Baking cookies
Cakes and apple pies
Never once questioning
The who, what, when, and why
No identification of
What this nation is facing
So, this poem is for you
This is a safe poem
For those who never
Challenge the status quo
As their status grows
They worry only about family vacations
Don't understand what the world
Is facing
So, this poem is for you
This is a safe poem
That will not make
You see the revolution
Or ask you for the solution
To end war or poverty
This is for the ones
That can't see the glass
Is half full or half empty
Because the reality
Is this
That the truth
Has been missed
As they continue to resist

And dismiss
And twist the lies so they
Can sustain
While they ignore the world's
Pain
This poem is for you
This poem will not talk about
The direction this country
Is going after the election
This poem will not talk
About injustice or inequality
This poem will not set
Your mind free
This is a safe poem
That will not create any storms
Ripples or waves
You will not have to be brave
Or will you be called to action
My reaction is to give you
What you want and
What you believe
That you need
That is
A safe poem

Who Is Going To Be The Voice?

Brown vs. the Board of Education
Was supposed to end segregation
In this nation but still today we are
Facing discrimination as assimilation
Continues to be the enemy of
People who look like me
3 nooses hung from
A tree
Began the controversy
But justice was light and lean
For those White teens
All of them were suspended and
Told to apologize
While the Black kids
Were all thrown in jail
Families unable to make bail
Mothers brought to tears
Because their sons are facing
Up to 22 years
As a White judge and jury
Have closed the chapter
On this story
We must fix this quick
And make it right
By bringing to light
The Jena 6
The Jena 6

And something must be done
About the one's carrying the gun

They are supposed to serve and
Protect
Yet, their actions remain
Unchecked
So now who is going to tell
The story of Sean Bell
Who died senselessly
At the hands of the NYPD

And Malice Green
And Sean Wilson
And Rodney King
And Jaime Jaurequi,
And Kim Grove
And George Floyd
And Brianna Taylor
And Michael Scott
And Aiyana Mo'Nay Stanley-Jones...et al

Who is going to be the voice
In the courts?
When justice can be bought
Who is going to be the voice
Of the Rutgers team
Who were living the
American Dream
Called out of their names
It is a shame
The times that we live in
I am hoping one day it ends

Dream

See
Martin had a…..
Nefarious has a …….
This generation
Does not have a …
Beneath a triple beam
I tried to live the American….
Selling crack to fiends in
Order for me to live out my……
The line between wrong and right
Is thin like the line that separates
Love and hate
But wait the weight of the world
Is upon my shoulders
Every day that I get older
My eyes see the poverty
Of those who will not ……
Their ship has run out of steam
No desire and no fire
Burning inside because something
In them has died
A man with no vision is easy
To manipulate
Because if nothing penetrates
His mind you will find
That he has no hopes or ……
See,
Martin had a ……..
Nefarious has a ……..
This generation does not have a ……..
Election stolen year after year
And the ones who are still here
Are complaining about the process

And those who have less
Have not voted so their voice
Is not heard like a bird
With no song to sing
They bring nothing
Just accept the hand that
They have been given
Only living for this
Moment in time
As their minds have given up
On achieving the ....
Selling out but
What exactly has been sold for
30 pieces of silver and gold?
Perhaps a savior or maybe your soul?
Because what is now broken
May never be whole
People marched back then
Because they had a......
Nothing to lose and everything
To gain
The issues and their political
Views are the reasons we
Are here but I fear that
This...will soon disappear

Still
Martin had a .....
Nefarious has a........
This generation does not have a........

The New Paradigm of Afrocentric Thought Process

When I say that the times
Have changed
I am being truthful and
Not sarcastic
When I say that the current
Paradigm of the Afrocentric Thought
Process has changed
I am being coy
Why?
Because some of us believe that
Enjoying the benefits of
A Lexus coated dream
Means
That we have indeed arrived
Yet, I say with deep regrets
That we have never left
I stand corrected
We have left our
Music like jazz and the blues
We have allowed our
Political views to be shaped
By MTV and BET
But for me that is only the
The tip of the iceberg
I say that we deserve
The poison fruit of
This Process
The New Paradigm of
Afrocentric Thought
Has you having
Your hand out
Asking for a handout
Has shaped and formed
Doubts in my head
Especially when I hear
The things you have said
Makes me think that we

Are still not equipped
To get off the slave ship
Why?
Because this new paradigm
Of Afrocentric Thought
Has made us complacent
Shiftless fools

Today we have no idea
About sit-ins
We only begin
To dive inside our
History in February
The shortest month
Of the year
And by now you are
Asking me what I want?
Simple.
For this New Paradigm
Of Afro-centric Thought
To change

How?
Don't behave like slaves
But rather be a part of the
Process
Don't rest until the
Dichotomy
Has been changed
Dare to dream inside
And outside of the box
Be an immovable rock
An anchor
Because in time
Only we can change
This Paradigm of Afrocentric
Thought
By first changing what
We believe in our hearts

Is It Necessary?

Is it necessary
For you
To discover
In February
My blackness
So, let me help
You with this

Black is
The absence
Of light
The opposite
Of White
But that doesn't
Describe me
Right?
All through
History
America insists
That we behave like slaves
Material gains are what
We crave
What can save
These jiggabos and
Jungle bunnies
It's not funny
Because that is how
They see
You
Me
We
Us

Hello Mr. Willie Lynch
A lot of what you said
Makes a whole lot of sense

Crab barrel mentality and
Lack of spirituality
Has a whole race blind
Losing their minds
Being raped from behind
Time after time
Africans have been
Brought to this land
From the motherland
No cultural identification
As slavery and assimilation
Has us facing annihilation
As Africa continues to shun us
Despising what we have become
As apartheid couldn't hide
The pride South Africans
Felt inside
Mandela was the fellow
That was locked up for
Nearly 30 years
So much bloodshed and tears
Civil disobedience
Is one of many ingredients
That helped a race of
People survive
I am alive
Because of
Rosa
Martin
Malcolm
Gandhi and others
In history
So, is it necessary
For you
To discover
In February
My blackness
So, let me help
You with this
Darkness is
The absence
Of light
While Black is
The opposite
Of White
But that doesn't
Describe me
Right?

Colorstruck

DOES **SKIN** COLOR REALLY MATTER?

Lord can you help me please?
I am down on my knees
It hurts so bad and It is so sad
That everyone's mind is stuck
The whole world is
Color Struck
Does it matter whether
I am light or I am dark?
It is what's in my mind
And in my heart
That counts
Not the number of zeros I have
In my bank book
It's funny cause most people focus
on money
And how you look
But when you look at me
What do you see?
I am not handsome
I am not pretty
But in the morning when I rise
I still have tears in my eyes
Every day I am alone I weep
Because my beauty is only skin deep
Color Struck
Accept me as I am
With all my imperfections
No corrections needed here
Do you hear me clearly?
My voice, my choice
It hurts me so bad and
It is so sad
You can't mold me and
You can't control me
For I will not be contained
You can't cause me any more pain

Maybe it was bad timing or
Maybe just bad luck
But anyone that looks like me or you
Doesn't have a clue
That you are now
Color Struck
My conclusion is an illusion
Because most people can't see
The real beauty inside of me
They let the media be their guide
Instead of their hearts
So many people are torn apart
Because now the world is
Color Struck

There Is An Old Can Of Paint

There is an old can of paint
That sits in a country store
So many times before
No one was sure if
The color was pretty
Enough to buy
Is this why
The lighter shades of paint
Were always bought first?
It hurts him so
To know
That the other colors
Have made it
As they all have decorated
So many homes
In this small town
Still he sits around
Waiting for someone to see
All of his possibilities

See, this can of paint
Ain't seen the light of day
Since he was made
There is no one to appreciate him
As his color starts to fade

Some say that he
Needs to be lighter
Others say that
His future would be brighter
If he changed his hue or
Will that confuse the issue?
And make it more complex
If he changes his color
Then what's next?

See,
In a world of colors
He still gets lost
As the people prefer
Flat or semi-gloss
Not realizing how
Pretty he could be
Because all they see
Is his exterior
Not the interior
Making him feel
Like he is inferior
When history shows
His color to be superior
In fact,
Black is
The basis for all races
But still he finds
That he is always
Last in line
In a world of color
He is like no other
As he still sits
Inside this country store
Wanting more
But getting less
Will he regress
Thinking that if he was lighter
Would his future be brighter
If he changed his hue?
Or would that confuse the issue
And make it more complex?
If he changed his color
Then what's next?

My Skin Is My Sin (Obamanation)

If my skin is my sin
Then this is where my story begins
And/or maybe ends?
In this nation we are
Facing history in the making
Although Obama's nomination maybe an
Obamanation for some
When it is all said and done
It is hand dipped in stratification
If he is selected and then elected
Sad to say he will go down in history
Like JFK
Still we pray that a change will come
Someday
But still our skin is our sin
As DWB is still a reality
As our Civil Rights are
Constantly violated
As cops are vindicated
Leaving communities
Struggling to understand
How and why 50 bullets were fired
Into an unarmed Black man
Those who supposed to serve and protect
Constantly have their hands around our necks
The nooses are no longer on the trees
But are the ones policing our communities
See, if my skin is my sin
Then this is where my story begins
And/or maybe ends

See in this weak economy
The elderly is pinching off of their pensions
Not to mention my 401k is getting

Smaller each and everyday
As the dollar continues to get weak
We need someone to speak

Because the future looks bleak
As McCain can't understand my pain
As bipartisan efforts continue
To fail as we are hoping
That the bail-out will work itself out
But I still have my doubts
Because banks continue to fold
The war in Iraq is getting old
And my skin,
Our skin continues
To be a sin

See,
Yesterday there was
Another dragging death in Texas
Should I expect this?
See,
I was born during the Sixties
I knew about the rallies and
The sit-ins
As we were trying
To win equality
Because today as it was before
We are demanding more and getting less
As we think that the world has progressed
When in fact it has regressed
While some say that I am blessed
Let me digress
And interrupt this flow
Allow Me to Tell U About
The America I Know

Hues

My hues give them clues
Some insight into my life
Because the absence of light
Means it is dark like my heart and
My skin
Take a look at what's happening
Every day they want to Freddie Gray me
So that leaves me paranoid
Something I can't afford
As they George Floyd me
As shots in the back make them
Michael Scott me
Nevertheless, they still think
Less of me
Right now I am calm, cool, and collected
Something that is never expected
From anyone that looks like me
As I am now reflecting still deflecting
These negative thoughts in my heart
Because it only takes a spark
To ignite the dynamite
Because I am a time bomb
Waiting to explode
As the only code to disarm me
Is equality
Nagasaki has nothing on me
As the instructions on self-destruction
Starts and ends with me
I am my own worst enemy
As the authorities don't knock
When they kick in my door
Makes this harder to ignore
Therefore,
Authorities are allowed
To Breonna me, legally
That is why it so unlucky
To die in Kentucky because
They fuck me constantly and consistently
On a daily basis as their racist behavior
Continues as the venue
Never changes as the events
Are meant to be played out
So I doubt that this will
Ever work itself out
As my writ to change was denied

As I am being tried,
I tried to explain my pain away
He couldn't be persuaded
Because the lies were
Dissuaded and covered up
The mistakes that have been made
That's why the judge wouldn't budge
So it made it difficult to get my story
In front of the grand jury
So I couldn't get a fair trial is foul
So they fear that a jury of my peers
Would acquit me
As jury nullification would be
The only thing to save me
Now they want to declassify the lie
Because when my people buy
They make other people rich
That's the only reason why corporations
Are uplifting the Black Nation
And jumping on the bandwagon
As they don't want the world to
See them dragging their feet
As they have done so many times before
They are still giving us less
But wanting more
Now they want to explore
Unity and Equality
Because now it is more profitable
To support minorities
Because in the end
It is more about the Benjamins
Then the color of skin

Unthinkable

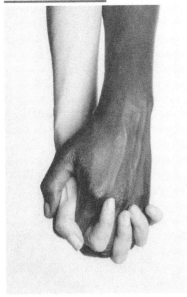

They say because
I am a 60's baby
That maybe
I shouldn't
Date you
And that
I should hate you
For all the things
Your ancestors
Did to my people
Still things are not
Equal
Segregation
Has this nation
In an uproar
Not sure
If we should
Add more
Fuel to the fire
But my desires
Has my soul on fire
Still I am uncertain
Cause we are flirting
With death
Would you take
Your last breath
To be with me?
Because history

Dictates
That hate
Is still an issue
That resonates
In this nation
As some still
Want reparations
For what America
Has done

Black and White
Might make gray
Still we are 50 shades
Away
Are we ready?
To do the Unthinkable
Just like Alicia Keys
A minor detail
Could cause us to fail
We have to B sharp
As we follow what's in
Our hearts
So many things
Can tear us apart
Could this be an
Afterthought?
To spark or ignite
The flame
Will they remember
Our names?
It is a shame that we
Can't change history
As we attempt to write a
New chapter and
A new verse
Are we ready for the
Hurt and the pain?
Nothing ventured
Nothing gained
Are you scared?
Are we prepared
To do what's in our
Hearts?
Will we let their
Hatred tear us apart?
This is the time for
Complete honesty
Would you die for me?

Or hang from a tree
So that we
Could be
Together
Have things gotten
Any better?
Still
Black skin is a sin
Because the man
That lives at
1600 Pen
Is a topic of hate
As many continue
To debate and are
Driven
Saying he's not
A U.S. citizen
When the real issue
At hand
Is that he is a
Black Man

See,
Our civil rights
Might get violated
Still we are hated
By some who
Frown upon
What we have done
Procreation adds
To the situation
That we are facing
Now is the time for
Complete honesty
Because honestly
Are we prepared
To see this through
To the end?
Maybe because
I am a 60's baby
I am scared
As people still
Stop and stare at us
In God we trust
Still Black and White
Makes gray
Although we are
50 shades away

I pray
For the day
Where skin is
Not a sin
Because
In moments
Of insecurity
Will you be there for me?
And give me the security
I need
Will you bleed for me?
I need to know right now
Because I have found
That 40 acres and a mule
Helped fuel
The separation
We are facing
In this nation
These ideologies
Can be detrimental
For you and me
Plus other factors
Still some want
39 and a tractor
Because it's been said
That at the very least
A mule is a stubborn
Beast
So to compensate
For the hate
For American Slavery
This should
Not be an issue
For you and me
Although the hate
Is still visible
Are we stronger enough
To do the
Unthinkable

Strange Fruit

I nod as I trod
Upon the sod
Because the grass roots
Of truth have failed to yield
Fruit because complacency
Is a Strange Fruit that is served
With lies and alibis because
Back in the days heroes and sheroes
Didn't wear mask
No disguises as they would ask
The difficult questions as the
Complexion of skin was a sin
That required a fire to be ignited
That now beckons us no more
So why fight it? What for?
Trinkets make us forget
As we thank our oppressor
For stimulus checks
Instead of dignity and respect
Understand that sleight of hands
And misdirection are all
Tools of magicians
So what's missing?
Hocus Pocus you need to focus
You are looking at the wrong thing
We no longer can sing
We shall overcome because
We believe in order to achieve

We must fall for any and everything
So now what's happening?
Rims spinning on the vehicle of change
Isn't it strange that icons are long gone
Only to be resurrected
In February as monetary gains
Failed to change the landscape
Again,
As I still trod on the sod
Because the grassroots of truth
Have failed to yield fruit but
I need to quit because
 I am a hypocrite that quips
With myself and not against
The status quo
Because I know that I am
Just a tired Knee-grow

My Nigga

Weeping willow weep no more
For your tears have been heard
Hitting the floor
And though my ancestors' blood
You have consumed
Their spirits still loom
Can't you hear them
Crying from the tomb?
My Nigga
No matter the shape or form
When it is said it performs
Negatively
On the ear drums
And for some
It embraces a race of people
That are not seen as equal
My Nigga
Even deep within the race
Some embrace
The term as a form of greeting
In gesture or in an informal meeting
My Nigga this and
My Nigga that
The fact is it is a negative way
To describe Blacks
One day we will learn
The negative connotations
Of the term
My Nigga

Obamanation II

Hilary lied as
Obama tried to
Cover his tracks
But he could not retract
What his mentor was
Teaching
In his church
But in the end
This may hurt
His chances
To be
The first Black president
Of this country
Still the democratic process
Is a mess
We first saw the flaws
In the sunshine state
By then it was too late
Because the push from Bush
Sent Al Gore out the door
Now in the Midwest
Inside the Buckeye State
The nation waits
As Republicans cross party lines
All in an effort
To undermine and
Split the democrats
In half
As they laugh
Bragging about what they
Have done
See,
McCain doesn't understand
My pain
And he can't bring back
All the lives lost in Iraq

Or the houses foreclosed on
Across this nation
He has no idea what I am facing
See,
When the money is funny and
The change is strange
Plans must be rearranged
Still the nation waits
For the
Super delegates
To decide
Still, will the will of the people
Prevail or will this process again fail?
As the great divide continues
What's next on the menu?
As the venue now turns to PA
To see which way
The votes will sway
For now, the lead is slim
As we head into June
Singing the same tune
That at best
There are still flaws in the
Process
As some votes may
Need to be counted
Again, and again
See,
McCain doesn't feel my pain
And if we don't fix
These flaws quick
Then what we saw
In the sunshine state
Will again seal our fate

Where To Begin

Not sure where to begin
So much I can write with this pen
Should I write about Katrina?
Still years later I
Hear you calling
I still hear the trees falling
Now the levees are dry
Why did so many people have to die?
Most of the people that look like me
Are still drowning in poverty
Searching for equality
As the push from Bush
Is just an exercise in futility
Still their hopes are wrapped up
In bureaucracy
See everything is in order
In the French Quarter
Up there you can hear the blues
Yet years later it is still news
Especially down in Ward 9 and 10
The people are still struggling
It is so troubling

Not sure where to begin
So much I can write with this pen

See my generation is the last
Because civil rights is a thing
Of the past
As this new generation
Has no idea what they are facing
In fact, they have no idea of what
It means to be Black and
What the movement for
Self-improvement was all about

As the Black Panthers worked it out
Pumping their fist
Shouting this:
Fight the power!
Fight the power!
Or the day Malcom
Was standing
In the window
With his AK
These are the heroes
That made a way
For us today
But look at us now
As I hang my head down
See,
The Million Man March
Was the last symbol to me
Of the things I have experienced
Growing up in this country
As I hope everyone knows
We have a long way to go
We have a long way to go

Not sure where to begin
So much I can write with this pen......

I Said That I Would Never Write Again

I said that I would not write again
But then my pen started reacting
To what's happening
In the sunshine state
Another victim of violence and hate
See in Alabama
They still call Obama
A boy
While White celebs
Think that Black
Babies are toys
At my age you wonder
How I survived
How am I alive
When my pants
Still sag and
My timbos drag
And on cold days
My accessory
Is a do rag and a hoodie
Still I
Don't understand it
The 32 Bandit
Wore a hoodie too
In the commission
Of his crimes
I find
That everyone
In their mind
Thinks that everyone
That wears a hoodie
Just like me
Is up to no good
Especially in
Affluent neighborhoods
But what you perceive and believe
Is rooted deep inside of you
See,
Hoodies might give

Way to stereotypes
That could end your life
But this is America and
You have the right
To wear what you want
And be what you want to be
Even if that accessory
Is a hoodie
So, Zimmerman thought
In his heart and figures that
A Black boy with a hoodie
Is a Nigger
Especially since the neighborhood
Was White and gated
He hated
The idea of segregation
Or integration
So, his answer to
The situation
Was to pull the trigger
Nevertheless, the slugs
Hit him in the chest
Now figure out this riddle
How dangerous is an iced tea and
A bag of skittles?
And why do we have to get outraged
For justice to be served?
When Zimmerman should get what
He deserves?
See
In Flo-RiD-A
They know how to
Get-Rid-of- YA
If your pants sag
And your timbos drag
And your accessory
Is a hoodie or a do rag
Just say so long
You too may be gone
Just like Trayvon

RIP Dedicated to Trayvon Martin

Why Do You Hate Me?

Why do you hate me so?
When I love you more than
You can imagine
More than you'll ever know
Why do you feel
The need to make me bleed
When all I ever wanted was you
Why do you beat me black and blue?

See,
I have loved you from my youth
But now there is a different truth
That I am facing when it comes to you
So,
Why do you feel the need to make me bleed?
Why do you beat me black and blue?
And tell me why is there so
Much anger inside of you?
Now I feel your hatred
Has graduated to this
Clenched fist against my head
Do you really want me dead?
You know that I would
Do that for you
So,
Tell me why you feel
The need to make me bleed?
And tell me
Why have you planted this seed
Of hate between us?
You are the one I love and trust

First it was with words
Now it is with your fist
What have I done to deserve this?

Nevertheless, I guess
There is a deeper truth that I can't see
When it comes to you and me

The 3 Laws of Newton and Kepler

It is hard to refute
Newton's truth
As many could not find
Flaws in the 3 laws
An object either remains at rest or
Continues to move at a constant
Velocity
More precisely, the first law defines
The force qualitatively
While in my mind
The second law offers
A quantitative measure
Of the force of course
As the third law
Asserts that a single isolated
Force doesn't exist
But the premise
Is a little bit faulty as
As apples do fall from a tree
At least that is the way
It happens today
In technology
Combine these with the
Universal Gravitation of
Kepler then you understand it
Better
That planetary motion states
That bodies in the Solar System
Have elliptical orbits
This is law number one
As the second law explains
That the closer a planet is
To the sun
The faster it moves
As the orbit of a planet is an ellipse
With the Sun at one of the two foci
Now I will try to apply these laws by
Introducing another Newton
To this and help me explain

This concept next
See
Huey P. Newton
Was a Marxist
A
Leninist
A
Social scientist with a
Socialist belief system
That society should
Be classless
With common ownership
In productivity
Given to all citizenry
As social and economic equality
Is the idea of a vanguard party
With state dominance over
The economy which is
In direct opposition
To capitalism and democracy
So now let's try to apply these
Theories in relation
To the social ills we are facing
In this nation
If justice is the sun
Then it takes longer for
Peace to orbit around it
But if injustice is stronger
Then it will take longer which
Omits Law Number two
And goes straight ahead
To Law number three
Which states that
The orbit's trajectory
Moves slowly so
The inertial frame of reference
Socially is no different
In physics or astronomy
As an object remains
At rest or continues to move
At a constant velocity
Unless enacted upon by a force
So now I suspect
In retrospect that there
Is scientific evidence
That will put this to rest
That a knee to the throat
Caused the Floyd effect

Killing all hope
Still we are in a state of flux
As they still have no love for us
As the speed of these
Velocities and atrocities
Against minorities' orbits
Constantly circles our mental skies
As the applied pressure from
The oppressor causes a stressor
Whose superposition will never
Rise as the juxtaposition
To equality will always
Be inert
As the center of gravity
Causes us to hurt
Because when we are standing
Hatred is used like shooting stars
Causing delays as our Milky Ways
Leak as we seek new paths
Because old formulas
Require new math
As we are so far from justice
As the substance of things
Hoped for dissipates
As there is no weight
Still we are forced to gravitate
As hate navigates our orbit at will
Still the fear of a Black Planet
Is not accepted and the reason
Why we are still disrespected
As theories on social justice
Are not widely accepted
And are heavily criticized
Because other theories
Revolve around and center
On lies

We Still Have A Lot To Learn

He who learns but does not think, is lost! He who thinks but does not learn is in great danger

You flood me with praise
When I write about trees
Or rivers, mountains and
The seas
But when I raise my fist
And yell that we need this
A revolution!
Your solution
Is to shun me with silence
When I speak up against violence
Again, you shun me with what?
Silence
When I say war no more
Because the reasons
In my mind I find
Are unclear
I find myself standing
Here
Alone
Facing my worst fears
Therefore, I try my
Best when I protest
That the
Truth as I know it
Beats all alone
In my chest
And when I perform
On stage and talk
About the men in uniform
They snap their fingers
At me
As a sign of unity
Because clarity is still a rarity

At least someone understands
The plight of this Black man
And others like me all
Across this land
When I speak out about
How they love baseball
In Cincinnati
They don't shun me
Because in this game
There is no umpire
To stop the pain
As Louisville sluggers
Are replaced with batons
As the beatings go
On and on
Long after the crowd is gone
So, in case you didn't know
The video is still playing
I can only imagine
What they are saying
Or what you are saying
And when a fellow poet Mali
Words speak directly to me
As he says
That they are still counting
The votes in Florida
As I agree
People start to run far away
From me and my poetry
When I say that perhaps
If there were no Republicans or
Democrats
We could interact and
Accept each other on
Our own terms
But
You know
And I know
As human beings
We still have a lot
To learn
We still have a lot
To learn
WE STILL HAVE A LOT TO LEARN!!!!!!!!!

Nothing Has Changed

Half tea and half lemonade
Being sipped in the shade
Dark skin being whipped
For mistakes that God has
Made?
While injustice flows down
The cracks of black asses
As blood mixes with blackberry
Molasses
Making a preserve that
Master feels we all deserve
As injustice is served
Via ropes, nooses, and chains
As Jim Crow is laughing
Over and over again
Because
400 years later
Nothing Has Changed?

Target

How much shit in my pamper depends
On whether or not my vas deferens is clogged
As my colon is swollen as my testes get tested
As they test me, as premature ejaculation yields
No satisfaction as stratification caused a reaction
Is nothing new because we knew as the nation grew
The discourse of our discontentment could
Never circumvent the continuous disappointment
As they conquer and divide us
As genocide keeps us oppressed
As we try to suppress our anger inside
As mothers continue to cry because
We are baptized by the lies
Only to realize that being Black
Simply means having a Target on your back

The Woodshed

They say the KKK
Lynched many Black souls
Threw them all in Black holes
Behind the Woodshed

Still it has been said
That many more Niggas bled
As they fled
Heading North of course
Bleeding and leaving
Behind the Woodshed

Still many women bled too
As their bellies grew
The lies did too
No one knew
About their dead
Behind the Woodshed

Whatever the reasons maybe
The Woodshed has earned
Its place in history

Children have been found dead
Buried beneath the Woodshed
They bled as serial killers fed and
Gnawed upon their bones
In the quietness of the night
You can hear them all moan
Cries of the undead and dead
Behind the Woodshed

See,
No one could save
The babies in unmarked
Graves
Born to men with different
Names who were ashamed
Of what they had done and
Worst what they had become
Sadly, it could not be undone
Fathers and daughters
Mothers and sons
Priests and nuns
Accidents with guns
Tongues cut out
By knives
It is no wonder why
So many lives
Couldn't survive
And are dead
Behind the Woodshed

Ungirly desires
Has his loins on fire
Man on man contact
Has him lying on his back
Scared of how he'll react
If he found out
That his son was gay
He prays that day
Never comes
As he succumbs
To the truth
That has haunted him
In his youth
It is why he fled
And sought out safety
Behind the Woodshed

The New Uniforms of The KKK

From Woodsheds
To Weeping Willows
To gallows in public places
Injustice follows, tormenting
Black faces leaving lipstick
Traces on the collar of inhumanity
As the unjust must atone for
The souls they sent home
As mothers weep alone.
Over the graves of their
Sons knowing the crimes
Against them can't be undone
It's hard to hum
We shall overcome
When you are numb
The Novocain of injustice
Wears off quickly
But bearing the pains of
Change may seem strange
Until you gum down on
The reality that in order
To get to the root of the
Matter
Lies have to be pulled out
As the cavities of racism
Have to be filled with Temperance
Love, and Compassion
As abscess has infected access
To equality
As incisions and other decisions
Must be weighed out
Against wounded circumstances

Stale beliefs and outdated
Methodologies of the 60's
As white sheets have been replaced
By three-piece suits
As they now
Meet in board rooms
As their
Rhetoric of hate still looms
As lone wolves howl across
The internet as a new threat has
Been born
As websites give
Insight and shed light
As their campaigns continue
To reign as they pop champagne
Because the boys in blue
Are doing what they use to do
Legally because brutality is now
Performed by these men
Wearing blue uniforms
Versus the white sheets of the past
Curses are inherited generationally
As they systematically
Try to exterminate and eradicate
So they can create the perfect race
But burning crosses on lawns
Is far gone and so are the sheets?
The new uniforms are being worn
By the ones patrolling the streets

Mr. Officer

Mr. Officer I mean you no
Disrespect
Soooooooooo
Why do you have your
Foot on my neck?
Aren't you supposed to serve
And protect, yet
Many in my community
That look like me
Are subject to police brutality
See,
You sound the alarm and
Cause us bodily harm
When most of the time
We are unarmed
In fact, it is just a crime
To be Black
Because
At any time, you could
Be shot in the back
So how should we react
To legal executions?
Do you really want to
Know my solution?
REVOLUTION....
See,
A broken tail light
Gives them probable cause
As you will probably
End up behind bars
If you are lucky
But how you react
Will determine if you get

Shot in the back
Eight times
As
I find that in itself
This is a crime
So if you ask me
It is murder
In the first degree
Malice, Intent, and Forethought
As the officer did what was in
His heart
Deliberation and Premeditation
Sheds light on the situation
Systematic Eradication yields
No vindication
As the courts continue
To support these sanctioned
Executions
As the only viable
Solution is
REVOLUTION!!!!!!!!!!!!!
See, I am
Fed up because the Feds
Overlook how many
Black men are dead
As the blood shed
Is caused by trigger happy
Cops
When will the legal executions
Stop?
Never,
Because things have
Not gotten any better
Since Obama was put
In the White House
Many want him out
But until then
Frustrations are being taken
Out on other Black men
When will it end?
The only viable solution
Is REVOLUTION!!!!!!!!!!

Black Lives Don't Matter

They attack Blacks
Making sure that the deck
Stays stacked
As they went to the motherland
To bring us into another land
Still many years later
We are still struggling
It's troubling
Can't you see the enemy is also
In me
As jealousy and envy
Pours out of my orifice
Just a little bit, I have to admit
That you won't pump your fist to this
As this migraine drives me insane
Still I bring the pain
Like Cypress Hill
As the blood continues to spill
My head is already on the
Chopping block and because
I won't stop and can't stop
Death by Cop is a reality for me
As the need to bleed feeds my
Righteousness
So I might just
Write and run with this
As the idea of dying
Consumes me daily
I can barely
Control the urges in my soul
Manifestation of my greatness
Has many hating up on this
As they are
Quick to dismiss this
Because it's a taboo

To even say this
I am crazy or Cray Cray
Because every day
I hear voices
Telling me my choices are
Limited in scope
Visions of my neck swinging
From a rope
I am suicidal and
Homicidal
As the anthem of
Death By Cop
Rings in my ears
No
Quelling my fears
I am
Yelling
I am here!
I am here!
Over here!
As religious fanatics
Are so melodramatic
Still my Illmatic is a classic
As my thoughts are drastic
Popping off in succession
Blowing my mind
Because it is like a 9-double m
Extra clip as I trip
Through this
Under the chin
This is how it will end
Gray matter will splatter
Only to shatter
Into little bits
Because shit keeps getting
Swept under the rug
And because
I am not allowed
To be that which I am
Eternally damned
Son of Sam
Psychotic episodes
Explode as I implode
Too many sixes in the code
A combo from Sandy Hook
Combined with Columbine
Got them all shook
Took so many lives

Only to survive
Because they be White
In reality, it occurred to me
That
Black Lives Don't Matter
And that is a fact

Black Lives Don't Matter II

A man dying, crying out for his
Mother softly but you can't
Hear his plea because the officer's
Knee is on his neck
So, what do you expect of us?
To just accept it and forget it
I don't think so
See, for me this is the tip of the
Iceberg as Mr. Floyd deserved
Better than that
He was killed because he was Black
He was less than not greater than
Or equal
This is another sequel that has been
Playing for over 400 years since
Our ancestors arrived here
It's a prelude, an interlude, an encore
Something that we have seen before
Now it's evident that your president
Forgot that he's a resident of
Chocolate City
Where the majority of the city
Is brown
Get up or get down
Look all around you but you can't
Because you're hiding in a bunker
After taking a photo op and
Using Federal Cops to clear the way
So you could take a selfie
Why people like me
Are dying daily and monthly
There's no denying as they
Are replying back to us with chokeholds
Choking the life out of Black souls

Still fractionalized
Never to be whole
As they are minimizing
Our value even more
So before we ignore this,
We must chant
This even more
Until we are weary
And sore
Black Lives Matter!!!!!!!!!!!!!!!!!

Black Lives Don't Matter Part III

Upon the wind the truth
Has been scattered
Many dreams have been
Shattered
Why?
Because it seems to me
That Black Lives Don't Matter

I can't change the
Color of my skin
But it appears to
Be a sin
As we are under attack
Because we are Black
So let's examine the facts
Trayvon is gone and
Michael Brown is too
As I knew that the view of the
Department of Justice
Is to consistently exonerate
As we are the targets
Of violence and hate
As we wait
We hesitate
Knowing we can't get
Support from the court
Thus, it is no surprise
Because right before
Your eyes
Many Black jurors
Believe jury nullification
Alleviates the situation
While some believe
The only viable solution
Is Revolution
Still,
Families dreams have

Been shattered
Why?
Because
Black Lives Don't Matter

See,
As a 60's baby
Maybe
I am thinking it's best
To picket and protest
But the civil unrest
Puts patience to the test
But this quagmire
Is why some take to
The streets and set
Things on fire
Looting and shooting is
Another reason for them
To shoot and kill us but still
Upon the wind
The truth is scattered
Why?
Because Black Lives Don't Matter

Orange Is The New Black

I did hand to hand combat
In the Iraqi sand and
Returned home
A drug addicted veteran with
Multiple illnesses that I am facing
I am still chasing Agent Orange
For doing this but that bitch
Doesn't slip and she never
Shows the mess
That is beneath her dress
She has brought many
Soldiers to their knees
And have killed many like me
With PTSD and STD's
Many pissing blood and puss
Schizophrenia makes us dangerous
Who the fuck do I trust?
Can't you see they've
Tried to get rid of us
As it's starting to rain
As the pain
Is causing my will to rot
Suicidal tendencies in me
As Death By Cop is my reality
And is the solution or maybe
Demonic retribution or
Divine revelation
But now the truth is this
As I piss out the truth
Only to realize this
I did hand to hand combat
In the Iraqi sand
Only to returned home
A drug addicted veteran
Now I am forced to do
Hand to hand transactions
Under the staircase

I am still trying to
Erase the mistakes
That I made
My fatigues no longer
Camouflage me
Now the enemy wears blue
Instead of white robes and sheets
This shit is way too deep
Orders coming from on high
Politicians in blue suits and red ties
Don't shoot until you see
The white in their eyes
These are the guys
I am stomping with my boots
They need to understand
I did hand to hand
In the Iraqi sand
Returned home a drug addicted
Veteran
Multiple illnesses I am facing
Still chasing Agent Orange
For doing this but that bitch
Doesn't slip and she never
Shows the mess
That is beneath her dress
She has brought many to their knees
And have killed many like me
With PTSD and STD's
That has many of us pissing
Blood and puss
Don't you know that
Schizophrenia makes
Us dangerous
So,
Who the fuck do I trust?
Can't you see they are
Trying to get rid of us?
Check your history
Because it feels like Tuskegee
All over again
Therefore,
It is hard to ignore that
Because of war
I am bipolar as my molars
Grind up the bullshit
As they are serving me
Poison in my cup
Now from what I can see

Orange Is the New Black
It is the color of my jumpsuit
Locked up because I spread
The truth something you can't refute
I did hand to hand combat
For Uncle Sam
In foreign lands
Only to return home
A drug addicted veteran

What Are We Marching For?

Rosa Parks gave the spark
To a movement for self-improvement
And many stood at the nation's door
To grab a piece of the dream in '64
Back then there was purpose and unity
As the movement lived on in our communities
So what happens when the speeches become silent?
And the only viable solution is to become violent
What happens after the janitors sweep up the debris?
Does the movement make it back to the community?
What happens to the lessons we claimed to have learned?
Like what bridges to cross and what bridges to burn
Like being a father to our daughters and sons
Like atoning for all the wrong that we have done
So what has happened to all of the glory and the hype?
What has happened to the light that once burned bright?
Where is that flicker? And where is that flame?
As our Civil Rights are going down the drain
Leaving me to ask these questions, like;
What happened to that spark that
Was lit by Rosa Parks?
And
Why do the marches of today, just fade and slip away?
What has happened to the 1 million men who stood in DC?
Who vowed to rebuild their homes and their communities?
What started off as a mighty wind, now has become a breeze
As complacency and assimilation has brought us to our knees
As our approaches today differ in many ways
It encroaches slightly on the successes of
Marches back in 1964
However, the biggest difference is back then

IS

We "ALL" knew what We Were Marching For

Inevitable

Someday will never come too soon
Because I know today that tomorrow
Will change its tune
Why?
Because it is
Inevitable

I was born
To be scorned
Being ridiculed
Only fuels
This fire
As my desire
IS
To be me
Is
Inevitable

Someday will never come too soon
Because I know today that tomorrow
Will change its tune
Why?
Because it is
Inevitable

So with tears
In her eyes
She watches
Me die

Why?
Because she knows
That my death is
Inevitable.

She tries to
Reshape and
Carve out a different
Destiny for me
But society
Has a different plan
For this dark skinned
Man

Inevitable

Tears will fill her pillow as
Sycamores and Weeping Willows
Will offer their limbs
To him

Inevitable

Some years too late
They will stop and investigate
The hate
But the life that was taken
Has been forsaken
And now is lost
She wipes her wounds
Only to carry his cross
Now
She labors in vain
As her heart bears the pain

Inevitable

Someday will never come too soon
Because I know today that tomorrow
Will change its tune
Why?
Because it is
Inevitable

.

Rope A Dope

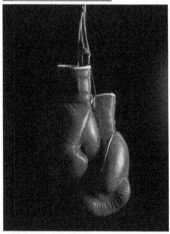

This Rope A Dope style was
Made famous by Ali
Bob and weave
As we bleed
What we need
Is for the referee
To call a fair fight
But we all know
That won't happen tonight
Or any other one
Because
He doesn't see the low blows
Right below the waist
It is a waste of time
For us to expect
That in this fight
To collect the respect
That is due
See,
The issue is the color of skin

When will this fight end
Round after Round
We get knocked down
But we keep getting
Up
Despite that the odds
Are against us
See,
The sanctioning bodies
Will have anybody

To do their bidding
No kidding
I am not
We keep taking
Shots in the back
All because we are Black
The deck is stacked
So,
Tell me
How are we supposed
To react
When in the ring of
Injustice they don't
Fight fair
Therefore,
They keep
Knocking us to the floor
It is not hard to ignore
That this fight is rigged
As they dig deep
Into our rib cage
The stage is set
Now we must
Watch the referee
Because he works
For the enemy
As he has the authority to
Stop the brutality but
He hesitates to give us a
Standing 8
No TKO's allowed
He has vowed
To let the fight
Continue
Because what they
Are serving on the menu
Is a plate full of hate
No hope as they got
Our backs against the ropes
We bob and weave
That will leave
The enemy tired
Eventually
As we bleed
What we need
Is a cut man
Who understands
How to cover up the bruises

Someone who
Chooses not to throw
In the towel but
Somehow
They still disembowel us
As
They still deny us
That I, myself, and me
Float like a butterfly and
Still sting like a bee
It is a natural reaction
When they are attacking me
I took that left hook
To the body and
It shook me
Their brutality
Made me want to
React violently
But the King said
That there must
Be a greater plan
For this Black man
To succeed
I will bleed
Because my creed
Is simple and plain
Turn the cheek
When I speak
Still they saw
That Right cross
To my jaw
That uppercut
Knocked me on my butt
But guess what?
I will keep on
Getting up
Because
This rope a dope style was
Made famous by Ali
The latest and greatest
Taught us how to
Bob and weave
As we bleed
What we need
Is for the referee
To call a fair fight
But we all know
That won't happen tonight

Split Decision

Every accomplishment begins with the decision to try.

Many were quick to jump with Trump
It's a fact that it is retaliation
For having a Black man as President
It's evident that Hilary had no chance
Because she didn't have a dick in her pants
No genitals
Plus no generals were going to
Take orders from a woman
Understand war is a man thing
So, now the pendulum swings in one direction
See there was no drama with Obama
Other than the color of his skin
So, it begins and ends with the fact
That this nation is still racist
Now this prez thinks
He is not impeachable
And that he's unreachable
Or untouchable
Like Elliot Ness but
Ukraine will bring him
So much pain
Like Hilary and her emails
The truth always prevails
Some put it up for sale

But I am not buying it
Because they all are lying
You have to admit
That the lies smell
As the flies
Fly around the bullshit
As Republicans know
What this is all about
As the House want Trump out
By any means necessary
It's scary
As the results vary
Now the Senate must decide his fate
As the Dems wait to get rid of him
Quick fast and in hurry
Eyes bloodshot
Vision blurry
The Senate is controlled
By Republicans
So, understand
That they will not remove
Him from the Oval office
Still they are
Quick to dismiss
The House's rhetoric
The witch hunt is done
Abracadabra
Hocus pocus
We've lost our focus
Blind to the truth
Why are we lying to the youth
Social Media got us tweeting
Meanwhile
Facebook still support crooks
Still we Pin our Interest
As Four Corners got us trapped
I am about to smack
The lies out of their mouths
You know what I am about
If you doubt
I am going to knock you out
Like LL or even better
Like Mayweather
Undefeated

Still
We've been cheated
Look at the score cards
Split Decision
You won't see this on your television
Because the lies make sure
That it is not televised
But the sound is coming
From the underground
Just like Harriet Tubman
I'm going to lead many to
The promised land

What We Want

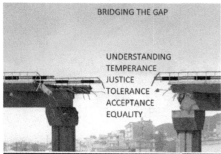

It is a fact that we must first
Bridge the gap between Blacks
And then we must settle on agreements
And similarities
Which is meant to erase the disparities
Along with the preconceived notions
That they have concerning minorities
While Blacks of different faiths and
Educational backgrounds
Must find common ground
As alliances are the keys to achieve
Equality and Unity
Along with political affiliations
Is vital in changing our situation
As our social and economic status
Are other things to build upon
But before we can move on
We must first accept our own
And be ourselves and
Stop pretending to be something
Else
Because the intolerance we have
About us hinders our progress
Nevertheless,
Our progress remains stagnated
As we are hated by both
Whites and Blacks
So, it is imperative to counter act
The status quo but we know
We lie when we do verbal drive-byes
Missing the point as we point out
Black on Black crime and aborting
Black babies both are a different
Kind of hate
Still they advocate for us
To return to our roots

While we denigrate
That because we don't
Know who we are and
That being Black is part
Of divinity the very core
Of `unity

I Won't Rest

I WILL NEVER REST
UNTIL EQUALITY IS GRANTED
TO PEOPLE OF COLOR
ALL LIVES MATTER ONLY
WHEN BLACK LIVES ARE FIRST
CHERISHED AND VALUED

NEFARIOUS J DORSEY

I am going to protest
March and Sit-in
I will not rest until injustice
Comes to an end
I will cross the picket line
Each and every time
I do not care what
Happens to me
I will die trying until
We are all free
I have been a soldier
Fighting in this war
Did not have any idea
What I was fighting for
Still I am going to Protest
March and Sit in
I will not rest until injustice
Comes to an end
I need Jim Crow to know
That we won't go
Quietly into the night
It is alright if I
Become a martyr
We must be smarter
This time
Because it is so much
Harder than it was before
Therefore,
We must approach
The situation differently
Still non-violently?
Until we are free

S.O.A.R

We got something to prove
Because if conditions don't improve
I will not hesitate to activate my faith
It is still the size of a mustard seed
So, If I need to make this mountain move
I will
Still,
Things continue to escalate
Because of hate
So, the need to make us bleed
Will not proceed
Because we need to exceed
Their expectations
Because what we are now
Facing is nothing new
Who knew that
In the middle of a pandemic
That systemic racism would rear
Its ugly head as many
Have bled for the cause
As losing life
For civil rights continues
As hate is on the menu
Because the
Appetite for Destruction is
Built on the construction of
Fear with instructions
That are easy to read
Because the design in their mind
Is to eliminate the Negro
We all know that Jim Crow
Changed his tactics and
It became more drastic
Then the Strange Fruit
That hung from trees

During slavery
Now their bidding is done legally
So, killing minorities
Is protected by the authorities
So free speech has failed to
Reach the majority
Because the fact that minorities
Are more likely
To die or be sent to jail
Simply means that democracy
Has failed on every level
As the devils learn new
Ways to burn Black people
Who are still viewed as not equal
However,
This is a different sequel
With a different cast
That won't allow you to put
Your foot up in their ass
They are quick to quip and
Tell you that I am
Not like my parents and
This is so transparent
That the looting and shooting
They will not avoid
Because they are paranoid
That what had happened
To George Floyd was a tragedy
A black eye on
The face of humanity
The insanity must stop
As crooked cops
Must be held accountable
As change and justice seem
Insurmountable
As
America must learn or
Burn down to the ground
The Sound Of A Revolution
Will be heard or
America will get what it deserves!

WAR

BLACK AND PROUD 2020 AND BEYOND

E
Q
U
A
L
I
T
Y

J
U
S
T
I
C
E

Navigate the hate
Only to retaliate
As their fear
Resonates in our ears
They don't want us here
All I hear is fear
All I see is that the
Majority uses and abuses
Their authority against minorities
Can't you see that my nationality
Is Black
But you can't see that
Because your knee
Is on my neck and
In my back
I can't breathe
Because you won't
Let me be
Because I am Black
You won't let me breathe
However,
I believe we need a reprieve
Because in order to achieve this
We must say it loud
Like James Brown did

I am Black and Proud
We need to chant this
Because they can't
Recant this
They are taking what
Little we've have
Soon
It will be a blood bath
So we need to bear arms
And start making bombs
So listen to what I say
Fuck the NRA
The right to bear arms
Is not just for White folks
So it is time to break some
Eggs and expose the yolks
As we continue to beg
For Equality
They are cracking our heads
As we are spoon fed lies
Scrambled truths
As the yolks are over medium
Never sunny side up
My views are fried with a side
Of grits and for dessert
A slice of shit pie may Help
As you taste all the crap
We've felt before
The message we need to convey
Should come directly
From Mr. Timothy McVey
As we refuse to obey
We will not be silent
Anymore
Can you hear the Uproar
It is no longer surprising
That our uprising
Needs to be upsized
Maybe a shake but
Definitely no fries
A New Order needs
To be created
Because we are hated
As we are still
Violated and Unappreciated

Uproar (The Next Chapter)

Sometimes I soar
But when I can't fly
I roar causing an uproar
Because my soul is sore
Don't know how much
More I can take
Before I break
I won't hesitate to take
The low road because I am
Ready to explode
Because the high road
Let's to many things pass bye
That's why when I look to the sky
I spread my wings and soar
But when I can't I roar
Causing an Uproar
All because my heart is sore
It is harder for me to ignore and
Turn the other cheek
When all I want is peace
So, I am trying to take a piece
Non-violently that is what
I am seeking so I must roar
Whenever I am speaking
I do so
Loudly and succinctly
So when I am yelling
Brevity is the key
So now can you hear me?

I am hard to ignore
Because when
I roar
I cause an Uproar
I am so serious
Because being glorious means
That violence maybe kneed-ed
In order to be victorious
That's why when I can fly
I soar
When I can't I roar
Causing an Uproar when
I am speaking
I am seeking peace
But if I must take a piece
Then so be it
Because if temperance
Doesn't fit
I will not quit or acquit
Even if I die
I must try to change it
Because equality means
Everything to me

Safe Poem II

You can relax
Outside your soul
You can play with
Other poets safely
You can take trips
Back and forth in time
And talk about the tree's
Beauty but not
About their bark
Or the lies that are
Hidden in their
Trunks
Without having to
Stop or yield
No cautions on
How you feel
No long poems
About social ills
Or short ones
That call you to action
Blank TVs refuse
To show you the
News because
You will be afraid
That your cooking
Shows would get
Interrupted
While Ferguson is burning
What you need is
Comfort from
Complacency
You need milk
That never spoils
Lies that are not
Bitter
And truths that
Are gentle to swallow
You need safety
From a poet like me
Someone
That doesn't cause you
Any ripples or waves
In your consciousness
Something you won't
EVER GET FROM ME!!!!
You need a Safe Poem

8:46

Dedicated to the memory of Trayvon Martin et.al

Made in the USA
Columbia, SC
28 July 2024

39422524R00050